MOMS NEED A BREAK

Written by Sarah Barstow and Illustrated by Ruth Mae Turner

Moms Need A Break by Sarah Barstow
Illustrated by Ruth Mae Turner
1st Edition

Summary: Babies and Toddlers are hard work!!! Sometimes Moms just need a break. This book will get you laughing at familiar situations & help you realize you're not alone.

ISBN: 978-0-578-76575-4

1.Parenting Humor 2. Mother & Child 3. Baby & Toddler Parenting Challenges 4. Humor 5. Mothers

This book is dedicated to all parents, especially these days when a global pandemic has made parenting even more complicated and stressful.

MAMA!

We hope you are getting the breaks you deserve and finding an occasional source of laughter in the antics of your kids.

Welcome to the world my darling little one.
Our journey together has only just begun.
I've never gazed at anything so beautiful, so sweet.
You've enhanced my life, made it complete.
I want to nibble your fingers & tickle your toes.
Each waking moment my love for you grows.

I will hold you for hours, keep you closely in sight.
Oh my! Did you just scream through the whole night?

Get the coffee going Mama. It might be a long day.
You're staying in your jammies, and that's totally okay!!

Can I run on no sleep? Is this Motherhood's first test?
Just once today, my love,
let your Mom get some rest!

You're growing day by day, even learning to crawl.
I will cover each outlet on every single wall.

We take tons of photos. . . and then we take more.
You're so very cute as you scoot across the floor.

Look at you: now you're even crawling outside.
Your skill and agility fill me with such pride.

You're a crawling master. It's what you were meant to do.
Ewwww!! Is that dog poo you
just cruised right through?

How disgusting! I guess I'll have to hose you down.

You've got to be the stinkiest kid in this town.

The poo is stuck everywhere. It's more than I can take.

Come on, dear child,

your Mom needs a break!

Walking is the milestone we've been waiting for.
    Time to get you up off our dirty old floor.

Uh oh! Walking quickly turns into running away.
    Surely there's a command to just make you stay?

Sometimes I'm just too tired to chase you around.
    Your energy keeps growing in great leaps and bounds.

So Mama is just going to
rest her eyes for a smidge. . .

Seriously? How did you get
on top of the fridge?

Hop up Mama. Time to look alert and stay calm.
I swear my eyes weren't even closed for that long.

My sneaky little one, I still think you're the best.
But just for a brief moment,

please give your Mom a rest!

You're mastering words by the hour- some sentences, too.
I shed tears of joy when you first said "Mama, I love you."
Our communicating relationship has finally begun.
Though not all your speech is proving to be fun.

"I want it." "No I don't want it." "No," you like to shout!
I need a degree in childhood psychology to figure you out.

Your tornado of emotions is turning me gray. . .

How long do toddler years last, did you say?

I need not fear ever forgetting my name.

"Mama." "Mama." "Mama."
It's always the same.

I heard you the first thirty times, for goodness sake.

I'm proud of you honey,

but let's give the talking a little break.

Sometimes I give in and put on a long show. And into the bathroom I quietly go.
To savor some quiet – some time that's just mine.

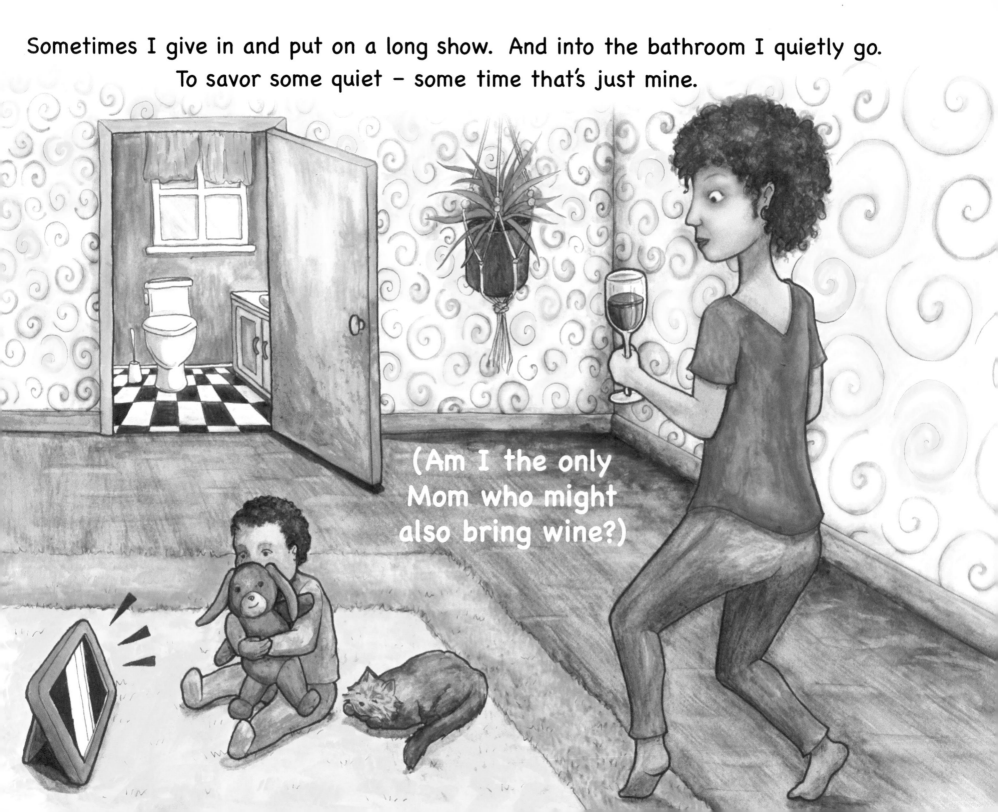

And then, feeling refreshed and ready for more,
I come out for tickles and giggles galore.

Though you're a whole lot of work, and the days can be SO long.
My deep love for you is beyond powerful and strong.

I love you so much, it makes my heart ache.
But please, now & then,
give your poor Mom a break!

Written by Sarah Barstow

Sarah always says that parenting is the "Best, Hardest thing you'll ever do!" Having a sense of humor definitely helps. When she's not navigating the waters of raising a toddler & a teenager at the same time, you might find her reading, hiking or turning a parenting challenge into a humorous book idea. 'Moms need a Break', is the second in a series of books which poke fun at some of the difficulties of parenting babies and toddlers. Her first book, 'Moms Can't Get Sick', is available on Amazon. You can also order directly from Sarah, and she will personally inscribe it for you.

Sarah can be reached at: theravenimage@yahoo.com

Illustrated by Ruth Mae Turner

The one thing Ruth has always known about herself, her whole life, deep in her bones, is that she is an artist. She is also a proud Mama of two courageous little humans. Professionally, Ruth has many years of experience with graphic and product design after earning a BFA in Industrial Design from MassArt in Boston. For close to a decade, she has handcrafted and sold leather wares under the name Rusted Antler Designs. She also loves to draw and paint, and has created many murals. Ruth strives to portray the dualities found in life through her work. There is no light without darkness.

May we all find the joy of balance, especially in parenting!

Follow her artistic journey @RustedAntler

Contact Ruth at: www.RuthMaeTurner.com

CPSIA information can be obtained
at www.ICGtesting.com
Printed in the USA
BVHW092056031120
592456BV00001B/6